To/
Bernie,
I hope you find
some of my war
comforting.

CU00671619

BE INSPIRED TO BE

Daily Inspiration

Belinda O'Neill

BOOKHUB®

PUBLISHING

Published by Book Hub Publishing, An Independent
Publishing House with Offices in Galway and Limerick,
Ireland.
www.bookhubpublishing.com
@BookHubPublish

ISBN: 978-1-7399578-6-5

INTRODUCTION

The journey to create this book of daily inspiration began in January 2017. Following a shock cancer diagnosis for a very close family member, I used my writing as a form of self-therapy, turning my anxious and worrying thoughts into more hopeful and positive ones. I set up my brand 'Be Inspired To Be' on social media, sharing some of my writing, with a view of helping others who were going through a difficult time. The response to my writing over the years has been humbling, especially through the Covid-19 pandemic and lockdowns, when I think we all needed a little extra boost of inspiration. Some of the work in this book you may have seen on my social media pages, and I hope you find your favourite.

It was during the most challenging of times that I discovered my passion and my purpose. I love to write, and I had a vision many years ago of writing a book. When cancer knocks on your family's door, it acts as a reminder of how precious life is and how quickly it can change. During this period, I fully awakened to *my life*, to pursuing my book writing dream. I asked myself 'If not now, when?'

It has taken longer than I initially anticipated to create, but like all good things, they take time. I have enjoyed the journey, it's a new experience for me coming from a finance background and it is time-consuming work, but it has been worth it!

My hope for this book, which is a combination of poetry, quotes, and reflections, is that it will inspire you to follow your dreams, your passions, and your purpose. When you are ready.

Be Inspired To Be,
Love,
Belinda.

This book is dedicated to my parents, Thomas and Maria, my husband Peter, and my son Leo.

Thank you for inspiring me, supporting me and for loving me.

ACKNOWLEDGEMENTS

Sincere thanks to my publishers, The Book Hub Publishing Group, especially Susan and Niall for their unwavering support and encouragement.

Thank you to Pamela Manson (The Donegal Artist), who took my vision for my book cover and created a stunning scene. You are truly amazing.

Thank you to my family, friends and social media followers for your kindness and support. A special thanks to Claudia, Catherine, Lisa, Maggie, Debbie, Ruth and Caroline for your valued opinions and advice when I needed them the most. I love you all.

Finally, a massive thank you to my parents Thomas and Maria, my husband and best friend Peter and to our wonderful son Leo. You kept me going when I doubted myself and loved me unconditionally, for which I am eternally grateful.

I^ST JANUARY

A new year, a chance to release
old worries and stress,
life is lived one moment at a time,
this year give every moment your best.

2ND JANUARY

New beginnings, lots of change,
multiple doors of opportunity will open for you
fill your mind, body, and spirit with the courage,
to assertively walk through.

3ᴿᴰ JANUARY

There will be moments which raise you up
and moments which will get you down,
know that a smile can always
be created from a frown.

Rejoice when times are good,
the low times will pass on
within is immense strength to get through,
the day, the night, and the dawn.

4TH JANUARY

Don't look back you are
not going that way,
stay centred and focused
only on today.

All you wish for
will enter when the time is right,
have a soothing January
rekindle your inner light.

5TH JANUARY

Never underestimate the impact of
impromptu acts of kindness,
they can instantaneously help
to release another's distress.

Showing that you care
can really change someone's day,
kindness can lift someone's spirits
in the most amazing way.

Be kind, always.

6ᵀᴴ JANUARY

Even through the dark skies
there is always a glimmer of light,
the clouds, they might hide it
temporarily out of sight.

Even though the light
it may be difficult to see,
the clouds they keep on moving
soon the sky will be cloud free.

7ᵀᴴ JANUARY

'Cherish'

Events happen which become
an awakening for us all,
momentarily life can change
with one single phone call.

Everything is temporary,
our earthly journey too,
cherish every second spent
with those closest to you.

8ᵀᴴ JANUARY

A cosy chair, a warm drink
a little time to peacefully think.

No hustle or bustle, time to clearly see
time to recharge, time to simply be.

9TH JANUARY

Sometimes silence is the bliss
that the soul desires.

10TH JANUARY

When you question
how resilient you are
remember you have made it
safely this far.

You are brave, you are strong
you are precious in every way,
be proud of the journey
and the person you are today.

11TH JANUARY

'These Days'

These days they can feel heavy
though the weight can't be seen,
it's carried deep within us
upon each other we often lean.

These days they teach us lessons,
we learn so much along this road,
it's connection with our family and friends
which helps us to offload.

These days they will lead us
to times much warmer and bright,
ahead are many clear blue skies
and mild and balmy nights.

12ᵀᴴ JANUARY

The stronger your mind
the more in control you will be,
through understanding your thoughts
the clearer you will see.

Release every thought
that is no longer positive for you,
be mindful of your circle
and of your environment too.

13TH JANUARY

'This Road'

This road we travel is filled with surprises and shocks
with many heartaches along the way,
sometimes there are no adequate words,
sometimes there is simply nothing to say.

The numbness it can be overwhelming
yet there is a greater story untold,
a pre-ordained pathway
we need to allow it to naturally unfold.

Our presence here is timebound
each moment is a gift in its own way,
make the best of your earthly journey
let gratitude surround you every day.

14TH JANUARY

'Be Grateful'

Be grateful for the people
who are always by your side,
be grateful for every experience
along this adventurous ride.

Be grateful every morning
as your eyes open to a new day,
be grateful for the love
in the home where you stay.

Be grateful for everything
give thanks openly for every blessing,
today let gratitude fill you up
today, allow no unnecessary stressing.

15ᵀᴴ JANUARY

Follow your true passion
be consistent and give it all you've got,
dreams can become reality,
pursue them,
never allow any circumstance,
to force you to stop.

16TH JANUARY

Do you ever wonder
how and when the self-doubt set in?
Those little niggles that chip away at you,
from somewhere deep within.

When this happens,
at some point it's likely that it will
remember why you started
you have an ambition to fulfil.

Flip your mind's script
you are a marvellous being,
allow your successes and achievements
to be the main images you are seeing.

Small incremental daily steps
will ensure you make the desired progress,
stamp out the doubt, reignite your confidence
your purpose requires you not to digress.

17ᵀᴴ JANUARY

You are doing your best
through these cold Winter days,
hold on, have faith,
brighter days await.

18ᵀᴴ JANUARY

'Emotionally Cleanse'

It's okay to be sensitive,
sometimes our emotions
need to be let out,
releasing them is fundamentally,
what a healing journey is all about.

Schedule time for an emotional cleanse.
Let any weariness go.
This important activity,
helps to calm and soothe the soul.

19TH JANUARY

'Every Moment'

As you reflect, you realise
that time goes by so fast,
it reinforces how important it is,
to relish every moment within our grasp.

Past events have brought many challenges
that no one could have conceived,
but here we are, time hasn't stood still,
time allows so much to be achieved.

Breathe in this very moment
feel it with every inch of you,
this moment is a wonderous gift,
every moment creates something new.

20TH JANUARY

Be kind to your mind,
because your body is listening.

21ST JANUARY

'Some Days'

Some days you feel like you could run a marathon
some days you could barely stroll a mile,
some days you grin from ear to ear,
some days you lack the energy to generate a smile.

Some days the sun is almost blinding
some days it hides away out of sight,
some days the rain it gently falls,
some days it pelts down, with all its might!

No matter what each day brings you
internally there is an ocean of power,
it will get you through all days, all weather,
even those annoying showers!

22ND JANUARY

Each day is a reminder
that in the sunrise there is hope,
in the mundane there is joy
and in every uplifting moment,
lies our most distinguished blessings.

23RD JANUARY

If you don't acknowledge how amazing you are
then others are unlikely to.
Step into your power,
pursue all that you desire
and believe in the miracle that is you.

24TH JANUARY

'Calmly Does It'

A deep breath in and out again
let the present fill you up,
calmly does it through today,
It's important to briefly stop.

When that overwhelming feeling
enters into your space,
it's a sign to pause and to breathe,
to really reduce your pace.

Calmly does it, focus on the now
everything will be okay,
try not to let the mind overthink
and wander beyond today.

25TH JANUARY

When you follow your passion with purpose
you are being authentically you.
The outcome may be uncertain,
but you will love all that you do.

26TH JANUARY

Friends, they can be many
or perhaps just a few,
irrespective of quantity,
they are a very special crew.

They listen, they support
they share lifelong memories with you,
friends, through challenging times,
they help you to get through.

27TH JANUARY

Do your best, it's more than enough
as juggling it all can be very tough,
create a list, take it one task at a time,
hydrate, take breaks,
know that you will conquer this climb.

28TH JANUARY

Recognise the light in others
never be afraid to shine your light for the world to see,
when we acknowledge each other's light,
the brighter our world will be.

29TH JANUARY

One moment at a time.
One thought at a time.
One step at a time.

Focus on the 'One'.

30TH JANUARY

When you find your inner calm
and you begin to let life flow,
your face lights up
with a mesmerising glow.

31ST JANUARY

The end of January it is now here
it can often feel like the longest month of the year.

These darker days can be arduous, with lots going on
yet, hope always rises with every new dawn.

May that hope surround you in the days ahead
may it be tranquillity this year, that you embed.

Concentrate only on that which you can control
let all the heaviness be set free, let anxieties go.

IST FEBRUARY

February, the month of new beginnings
the month when transformation occurs,
allow the old to swiftly disperse,
graciously walk through impending new doors.

Nature it stirs after a winter of hibernation
it's ready to sprout with the changes of the season,
it's time for you to know your worth,
your talents were gifted to you, for a special reason.

2ND FEBRUARY

When you look back on the
many miles you have travelled,
the story of your life
it becomes unravelled.

Every mile gave you the tenacity
to keep going,
reigniting your determination,
to keep growing.

Those miles have shaped
the precious being that you are,
those miles will ensure that
you will continue to go far.

3ᴿᴰ FEBRUARY

Each footprint you make
leaves an eternal legacy,
use those footprints to lead you
towards your destiny.

4ᵀᴴ FEBRUARY

'World Cancer Day'

Today we remember all the lives
that Cancer has cruelly touched,
the survivors, the patients, the families,
those we have lost and miss so much.

We give thanks to all who work consistently
to combat this awful disease,
we hope that in our lifetime,
suffering due to Cancer will cease.

Today let us offer a thought, a wish
let us reflect in our own way,
united we send out all those offerings,
on this 'World Cancer Day'.

5TH FEBRUARY

Sometimes you are ready for something new
for something that will totally fulfil you.
This earthly experience is too short to simply coast
we only get one chance at it, we must do our utmost.

Make the best of every opportunity
that the Universe sends your way.
It will enable a deeper sense of gratitude,
of your accomplishments, each day.

6TH FEBRUARY

Through extraordinary times
it's imperative that we nurture our minds.

Our health and wellbeing need our daily attention,
self-kindness is essential to aid burnout prevention.

Our mental and physical health are intrinsically linked,
it's important to be conscious of how we think.

Analyse your thoughts, let the self-rejection go,
aim to stay present, it's okay to take it slow.

7TH FEBRUARY

Believe in all that you are
all that you have ever been
and all that you are destined to become.

8TH FEBRUARY

Life is like a rollercoaster, or a roaring wave
it takes strength and courage to
remain positive and brave,
just remember you are never alone
we are all here, walking each other home.

9ᵀᴴ FEBRUARY

Ambition is never time bound
you can change the course of your life
as often as you see fit.
You have the lead role, and you are
writing your own manuscript.

10ᵀᴴ FEBRUARY

'You Provided the Light'

You may not always feel it
and you may not always know,
so many, they are grateful they have you,
even though it's not always on show.

Make peace with the past and forgive often
allow your love to radiate bright,
through the darkness and the smoky haze,
for many, you provided the light.

11TH FEBRUARY

Even if at times it feels like you can't
know that deep within you can,
back yourself, proceed with your plans,
convert yourself into your biggest fan.

12ᵀᴴ FEBRUARY

'Give Thanks'

Give thanks for the sun
which rises as you do,
give thanks for nature which
evolves and blooms.

Give thanks for the people who
help and support you,
give thanks for the memories gained
through all that you do.

Give thanks for every opportunity
to learn and to grow,
give thanks for all that you are,
you are loved more than you know.

13TH FEBRUARY

'Face Those Fears'

Face those fears which subtly
creep into your mind,
believe that as you step through fear,
success is what you will find.

Those fears they seek to hold you back
it's resistance which fuels doubt,
create some meditative space,
let those doubts and fears out.

Stay centred and clear on your vision
sense the happiness that floats all around,
know that when your intentions are pure,
contentment, it is found.

14TH FEBRUARY

'St. Valentine's Day'

St. Valentine's Day, an annual day
to completely celebrate love,
may it flow through our hearts and homes,
not forgetting our loved ones above.

Today, be sure to say, 'I love you'
to those who mean the world to you,
let love be your guide throughout today,
in all that you see, feel, and do.

15TH FEBRUARY

'The Other Side'

As you emerge from the storm
safely on the other side,
you will reflect in awe of your strength
and smile with pride.

That newfound strength will
continue to be your guide,
now overtly aware of
every onward stride.

16TH FEBRUARY

Unclench your jaw
let your shoulders slowly fall,
release that tension across your neck,
which can feel like a tight ball.

Close your eyes, steady your breathing
for a moment or two,
from your shoulders down to your fingertips,
let all the tightness trickle out of you.

17TH FEBRUARY

The little peak of sunshine
provides a subtle warmth upon your back,
it offers reassurance, those brighter days
they are on track.

It gently lifts your spirits
much needed at this time,
you breathe in that fresh, clear, cool air,
it really feels sublime.

Spring is almost in the air
soon we will see,
the magic of the Universe
through nature's changing beauty.

18TH FEBRUARY

Love and friendship are two
timeless, priceless and
precious possessions.

19TH FEBRUARY

The more seeds you lovingly sow
the more opportunities
with encouragement will grow.

20TH FEBRUARY

Sometimes taking a
short self-care break
is the most productive decision
that you can make.

21ˢᵗ FEBRUARY

'Love and Light'

Each day acknowledge your
own love and light,
it's within you even though
it's out of sight.

When your energy is low and
you are unsure of how you feel,
focusing on your love and light,
will help you to self-heal.

Meditate, relax,
be still for a time,
let your mind, body, and spirit
once again realign.

22ND FEBRUARY

Life is not easy
we are here doing our best,
all those daily challenges,
they are our resilience test.

We create powerful energy which
produces much needed light,
keep going, keep illuminating,
greater times, they are in sight.

23ᴿᴰ FEBRUARY

As you fully open your eyes and your mind
to all the wonderment that you see,
you inhale how immense it is
and you slowly begin to feel free.

24TH FEBRUARY

The Universe has a majestic way of
answering our deepest desires,
keep dreaming those dreams,
clearly visualise them,
then be prepared for how they
gradually transpire.

25TH FEBRUARY

Answer the true calling
that's inside your heart,
take a leap of faith
and make a start.

There are so many who are
waiting just for you,
believe in yourself,
in all that you are and
in all that you continually do.

26ᵀᴴ FEBRUARY

When you close the door to toxicity and
open it only to authenticity,
the more contented you will be.

27ᵀᴴ FEBRUARY

Wherever your journey
leads you today,
may kindness and compassion
greet you along the way.

28TH FEBRUARY

A new month is ahead
positivity is in the air,
new opportunities, new occasions,
new memories to share.

Great times await
there is no need to feel fear,
we are entering the growth phase,
of this brand-new year.

Out with the old
in with the new,
be prepared for the blessings,
that are heading to you.

29TH FEBRUARY

A special date which arrives
every four years,
may it be as special as you are,
filled with laughter, joy, and cheer.

1ST MARCH

Hello March, as you evolve
you give us Spring,
it's time to get ready
for the changes you will bring.

Everything happens
for a valid reason,
we welcome all that appears,
throughout this new season.

2ND MARCH

'Life is Like a Timeline'

Life is like a timeline
we never know exactly how
far we are along it,
aim to love, to laugh and to smile,
to really relish every minute.

Past events have shown us,
how fragile that timeline can be,
for time is our most valuable asset,
spend every second wisely.

3RD MARCH

What is it that you wish to do?
As your journey unfolds,
what really enlightens you?

The answers are within, waiting to be unleashed,
don't hesitate, you deserve happiness,
and above all, inner peace.

4ᵀᴴ MARCH

When the happiness in your heart
transpires to your face,
you know you are in
quite a magical place.

5TH MARCH

Never allow anyone's perception of you
to hold you back,
shake it off, keep going,
you are on the right track.

Everyone is carrying weights that we
know nothing about,
a little empathy goes a long way,
we are all trying to figure things out.

Don't regress, maintain progress
you are doing amazingly well,
your story of endurance,
will be a tale you can proudly tell.

6TH MARCH

Step out of the perceived shadows
and into your own light,
allow your individual vibrancy
to shine dazzlingly bright.

7ᵀᴴ MARCH

It's not easy to go centre stage
yet what's worse is not turning the page,
silence those whispers that question your worth,
move forwards and confidently, step forth.

8TH MARCH

'International Women's Day'

Together, united we are an
amazing source of energy,
let's empower and support each other,
to continue to increase our synergy.

We have survived a time
like no other before,
let this enhanced resilience guide us,
through brave new doors.

Let's challenge for change in every room
like the flowers of Spring,
let us all stand tall
and effervescently bloom.

9TH MARCH

'Tingles and Tears'

The tingles we get assures us,
unwavering protection is always near,
those tingles can bring on emotions,
quite often even a tear.

Those tingles and tears remind us,
that we are supported from above,
they are like a comforting blanket,
containing only divine love.

10TH MARCH

Within every personal story
is a little drop of pain,
a challenge, a shock, a loss,
requiring you to take a deep breath in.

Although it wasn't easy
you navigated your way through,
not allowing any of the situations,
to hinder or define you.

Within your story are remedies
that can help people near and far,
sharing your story is healing,
helping to mend those internal scars.

IITH MARCH

The more time you spend
with precious people,
the more precious
those people become.

12ᵀᴴ MARCH

Like the swirls of the ocean waves
or the roar of high winds,
there's an invisible force at work,
greater than everything.

That force of energy is within you
and all around you too,
trust it to guide you and inspire you,
in everything that you do.

13ᵀᴴ MARCH

We are not here to merely survive,
we are here to make a difference
and to phenomenally thrive.

14TH MARCH

Don't allow the ego to dictate
try not to procrastinate,
instead, back yourself and have faith.

15ᵀᴴ MARCH

A little advocacy, care, and support
they go such a long way,
perhaps much more than
words can say.

Through life, we all need
those who help us to rise,
that kindness to the recipient,
is the most majestic prize.

16ᵀᴴ MARCH

We do what we feel
is right at the time,
some parts of the journey
are complex to define.

Embrace each day with clarity
on all you wish to pursue,
what is destined to appear
will find its way to you.

17ᵀᴴ MARCH

'St. Patrick's Day'

St. Patrick, we ask
that you heal our sorrow,
help us to be present in today
and be optimistic about tomorrow.

Bless us with your shamrock,
replenish our faith, hope, and love,
send us down lots of luck,
from the Heavens above.

Today let music and memories
set our hearts alight,
from all our woes St. Patrick,
give us a little respite.

18ᵀᴴ MARCH

We all need a little sunshine,
a little warmth, a little ray,
it's mesmerising watching the sunrise,
as it welcomes a new day.

We can learn from each sunrise,
another chance to follow our heart,
don't worry about the intricate details,
simply make a start.

A year from now the sun will still rise
may you rise with it too,
tune into faith and bring to life,
those dreams embedded inside you.

19ᵀᴴ MARCH

There's a wonderful world
waiting to be explored,
don't hide your plans and ideas
behind closed doors.

You are only here once
let your imagination freely flow,
you will be astounded at how far
your ambition and vision can go.

20ᵀᴴ MARCH

'International Day of Happiness'

Keep calm, stay wise, be kind,
take each day, a moment at a time.

Self-care is important, make time for you,
when you feel good, your happiness shines through.

Focus on the now, invest in all you love to do,
may love, light and joy, forever surround you.

21ST MARCH

Think good thoughts,
do good deeds,
look for the blessings,
whilst sowing good seeds.

Create goodness,
inside and out,
that's what this journey
is all about.

22ᴺᴰ MARCH

The road we travel
has many bends,
our navigators are our
family and friends.

Earth angels surround us
with a welcoming glow,
aim to acknowledge them
as you go.

Show love and kindness
to those you hold dear,
those memories will ensure,
they are forever near.

23RD MARCH

If you are courageous enough
to follow the rainbow,
you will eventually find your gold.

24TH MARCH

'Breathe'

Breathe, you don't need to
conquer every ambition today,
a little step forward
is perfectly okay.

Go gentle on yourself,
know that you are doing great,
breathe, take it slow,
good times await.

25ᵀᴴ MARCH

Yesterday is gone,
today is where we live
and tomorrow can only
ever be wished for.

26TH MARCH

Time spent outdoors
in the fresh, clean air,
reawakens that inner
vibrant flare.

27ᵀᴴ MARCH

To function at your best,
it's essential to rest.

28ᵀᴴ MARCH

When you feel your heartbeat racing
and anxiety is setting in,
it's fear trying to hold you back,
from a purposeful new begin.

Take a few deep breaths, reset yourself
trust in every intuitive step you take,
your future, it is in your hands,
it can be all that you wish to create.

29ᵀᴴ MARCH

With a positive attitude
and daily gratitude,
you can achieve a magnitude.

30ᵀᴴ MARCH

Believe in the magic which trickles through you
from your mind, around your body,
to your fingers and toes.

A one-of-a-kind type of magic.

31ST MARCH

The third month of the year, closes today
regrowth is now in full swing,
the colours, the blossoms, the melodic birds,
they collaborate to produce Spring.

The energy feels lighter, smiles are plentiful
there's a hint of warmth in the air,
inhaling the landscape instantly transports you,
without you physically travelling anywhere.

Those brighter days we longed for in Winter
thankfully they are now here,
may the skies be blue, and the strolls be long,
let every internal blockage now disappear.

IST APRIL

'Compassion'

We all need a little compassion
perhaps never more than the present time,
energies are heightened,
our feelings are complex to define.

Together we can make a change
if we choose compassion over hate,
by accepting one another,
a thriving community we can create.

2ND APRIL

'Home'

Home, a place to relax and
to clear your mind,
your chair, your pillow,
your space to unwind.

It's where love and joy
fill every room,
where family gathers
and laughter booms.

Every nook tells a story,
you never feel alone,
no matter where you wander,
there is no place like home.

3ᴿᴰ APRIL

Daily life can get busy,
it can be all go, go, go,
it's okay for life to quieten
and to let life gently flow.

4TH APRIL

'Angels'

Angels they are around us,
they are there to support us with any burdening task,
they are always ready, willing, and able,
all we need to do, is ask.

5TH APRIL

The sun, the moon, and the stars
they are jewels that adorn our sky,
they proudly beam and twinkle,
never afraid, bashful, or shy.

Take inspiration from them
step onwards with your head held high,
it's time to leave old wounds in the past,
to fear, it's time to say goodbye.

6ᵀᴴ APRIL

'Your 90-Year-Old Self'

Imagine the conversation,
what is it you would say?
That conversation is important,
it could reframe this new day.

Picture your 90-year-old self,
what words of wisdom can you hear?
It's likely to be 'seize the day and
the path ahead is clear'.

Keep that image in your mind
when inner doubts begin to appear,
imagine your 90-year-old self,
whispering encouragingly into your ear.

7ᵀᴴ APRIL

'World Health Day'

World Health Day, a day to recognise
the importance of our health,
reinforcing that our health,
is indeed our greatest wealth.

Our health care workers are warriors
whose compassion is always on show,
today we give thanks for all they do,
to help us to recover, prosper and grow.

Our healthcare system in vital
we all rely on it in different ways,
everyone deserves access to healthcare,
on World Health Day and every day.

8ᵀᴴ APRIL

Open your arms,
welcome forgiveness in,
release every hurt,
every burden within.

Not everyone will care
as deeply as you do,
by showing mercy and compassion,
you will restore the calmness in you.

9ᵀᴴ APRIL

It's through a thought
that every good idea is conceived,
with our whole self we must believe,
through action, ambition, and passion,
our best life outcomes, can be achieved.

10ᵀᴴ APRIL

An off day, is just that
a day when we go into our shell,
it's our restorative place,
knowing that outside, all is well.

Days like these reset us
it can be much needed thinking time,
our inner energy gets refuelled,
so we can continue with the climb.

Remember these days are important
they are time out so we can rest,
to reach those goals we have set ourselves,
requires us focused and feeling our best.

11TH APRIL

The journey can be bumpy at times
fatigue, it can be hard to shift,
a step outside into nature
it gives us a much-needed lift.

There's no need to rush or to be forceful
take a little time to focus on you
make yourself a priority,
self-kindness is important too.

12ᵀᴴ APRIL

Radiate all that is positive,
loving and true and
that's what will be reflected,
back to you.

13TH APRIL

When you give thanks for all
that you are blessed with,
you will find that the good outweighs,
everything you are stressed with.

14TH APRIL

When 'you' truly love 'you'
only that quality of love,
will ever do.

15ᵗʰ APRIL

Life is love and loss combined
the two forever threaded
and intertwined.

It's a blessing to have
love beyond measure,
family and friends,
are a lifelong treasure.

Life is for living
every moment it is true,
tomorrow isn't promised,
today belongs to you.

16ᵀᴴ APRIL

Step outside,
feel the earth below your feet,
reconnect to your breath
and to your own heartbeat.

Awaken to the magic
of the world that you see,
allow the present in,
right now, totally be.

17TH APRIL

We are diverse human beings
each with our own spectrum of feelings,
be gentle with yourself,
allow inner healing.

18ᵀᴴ APRIL

'Light'

Within us is a powerful light
the more peaceful we are
the brighter it glows.
The world needs your light,
be sure to let it show.
Shine it like a beacon,
everywhere you go.

19TH APRIL

Even if you get consumed with doubt,
pursue, persevere, in the divine right time,
everything will work out.

20TH APRIL

If you measure success on the
possessions you have,
fulfilment you will never know.
If you measure success on the
blessings you have,
abundance in all forms,
will continually flow.

21ˢᵀ APRIL

'Dear Mirror'

Dear mirror, you show me my reflection
you highlight the physical me,
what lies beneath the surface,
dear mirror, you cannot see.

Dear mirror, you show me ageing
every curve, every line you define,
you highlight the life I've lived so far,
within this body of mine.

Dear mirror, keep on reflecting
in front of you I stand,
I hope I will always smile into you,
and appreciate all that I am.

22ND APRIL

'Earth Day'

Earth Day, a day to recognise and appreciate
this precious planet in which we stay.

The natural beauty it gifts us,
it can be seen everywhere,
it deserves our attention,
our tender love and care.

It's our home, our habitat,
part of us from our birth,
we need to make a concerted effort,
to protect and preserve our magnificent Earth.

23RD APRIL

Feeling emotional is perfectly okay
when it comes to emotions,
it takes courage to share,
we are human, we are sensitive
and our emotions,
show we care.

24ᵀᴴ APRIL

'Slow Down'

Slow down, life is not a race
stop and breathe, reduce your pace.

Life can only be lived one moment at a time
have faith that all will work out fine.

Focus on the present, the gift that is you,
gratitude, calmness, and peace will see you through.

Slow down, life is not a race
be gentle with yourself, reduce your pace.

25ᵀᴴ APRIL

'New Beginnings'

New energies, new beginnings
they eagerly await you,
with self-belief and purpose,
confidently step through.

You've changed, you've evolved
remember you are gifted,
it's time for pre-conditioned worries,
today to be lifted.

Get ready, get set
off you bravely go,
new beginnings will reward you,
more than you presently know.

26TH APRIL

What we carry in our minds
can feel immense,
it's through self-awareness,
self-care and through talking,
that healing can commence.

27ᵀᴴ APRIL

'Note to Self'

I pull on my imaginary armour
I let all negative vibrations rebound,
my mission is to protect,
this inner peace I have found.

Only I can control
my thoughts and my emotions,
no longer shall my tranquillity,
be compromised or stolen.

I choose me above everything else
that uncontrollably enters my space,
I set the tone and the sentiment,
this inner peace, I fully embrace.

28ᵀᴴ APRIL

May all shadows fall behind you
as you walk towards your brand-new start,
emotional as it can be,
you've made the correct decision to depart.

We only ever regret, the chances
we fail to take,
with your torch-bearing abilities,
a brighter future you will make.

29ᵀᴴ APRIL

As our world learns from past events
a more positive future will unfold,
all events are the future stories,
which for generations shall be told.

We are writing history
we all have a key role to play,
we need to feed our inner goodness
every minute of every day.

30ᵀᴴ APRIL

Life is a journey
to be lived a moment at a time,
some days they run like clockwork,
others are like a mountain climb.

It takes bravery and courage
to reach the mountain top,
when you reach the summit,
you'll be glad you never gave up.

Beauty surrounds us, in the sky
green fields and sea,
to the love we share in our homes,
which flows through you and me.

Even through the darkness
a flicker of light appears,
it reminds us that nothing is permanent,
it helps dissolve our inner fears.

With hope in our pocket
joy is never far away,
know that all will work out fine,
all will be okay.

Life is a journey
it evolves day by day,
step onwards with confidence,
trust your instinct to guide the way.

1ˢᵀ MAY

The past it doesn't define the present
life is not infinite, let's make it pleasant.

Allow all drama, to slowly drift away
let it be an optimistic month of May.

2ND MAY

There's something new to be
discovered in every day,
new memories, which in our heart,
forever stay.

Acknowledge those memories and
all the joy that they bring,
those memories rekindled,
continually make your soul sing.

3RD MAY

Love is a powerful gift which we give and we receive
a gift that through all storms, helps us to believe.

Never doubt the love that is around you
it's real, it's buoyant, it's authentic and true.

Where there is love there is light, keep the faith
many more great times and adventures await.

4TH MAY

When you are self-kind centric,
kindness becomes your new metric.

5ᵀᴴ MAY

Today, a new day, a new sunrise,
another chance to grow,
a new day to appreciate all that you have,
for gratitude to freely flow.

Steady steps forward are totally fine
remember today is a present
and there is no better present
than this moment in time.

6ᵗʰ MAY

'Self'

Self: It is our beginning and our end,
amazing and powerful,
greater than we can comprehend.

We have only one 'self', one chance to be,
one life journey in this world to see.

Self: It is who you eternally are,
emit your uniqueness,
let it be seen from afar.

7ᵀᴴ MAY

You can be mature but not old
you can be wise yet still learning,
you can be witty yet serious,
you can be happy yet still yearning.

You can be anything that you wish
at any given time of the day,
simply be you and never worry,
what others think or say.

8ᵀᴴ MAY

We all have it within us
to feel totally free,
as free as a bird
soaring over the sea.

As we release our worries
our inner blockages go,
the path becomes more tranquil
and new energy begins to flow.

9ᵀᴴ MAY

The trials of today
deliver the triumphs of tomorrow.

10ᵀᴴ MAY

Approach life softly,
no blame,
just acceptance.

11TH MAY

'Courage'

Courage is manifested through the daily steps we take
through every tough decision, we have had to make.

A soft whisper telling us, to trust a little more
assuring us that we can open, an abundant new door.

Courage is that little voice, our unique intuition
mute the doubt and to the courage, always listen.

12ᵀᴴ MAY

Be kind to everyone who enters your life
everyone has face challenges, pain, and strife.

Kindness is how we show that we care
always be loving, compassionate and fair.

Sprinkle kindness, with every footprint you make
through kindness a brighter world we will create.

13ᵀᴴ MAY

'Self-Fulfilment'

Self-fulfilment takes practice to be achieved
the foundation is to totally self-believe,
ignore any negative experiences of the past
you are precious and your talents are vast.

When you believe in yourself
the more contented you will be,
self-fulfilment is inside you,
confidently turn your self-belief key.

14ᵀᴴ MAY

We all have a purpose,
that is why we are here,
it can take a little time
for our purpose to become clear.

It can evolve as we travel
as we mindfully grow,
it's our divine mission,
that only we know.

15ᵀᴴ MAY

Life can get busy
with so many chores to do,
remember there
is only one of you.

It's sensible to take it easy
all will be okay,
the chores will get done,
be gentle with yourself today.

16TH MAY

Be proud of the daily steps forward
that you take,
be proud of the positive difference
that you continually make.

17ᵀᴴ MAY

Be the one who lights up the skies
be the one who lifts others as they rise.

Be the one who sees no boundaries
to what can be achieved,
be the one who knows success happens,
when we truly believe.

Be the one who can see their own greatness
even when a fog of doubt appears,
be the one who steps forward with faith,
not caving into fears.

Be the one who loves
with every ounce of their being,
be the one who helps others,
to express how they are feeling.

Be the one who sees the beauty
which this world gifts to us all,
be the one who never gives up and
who catches others when they fall.

Be the one who lives life to the fullest
who shines for the Universe to see,
be the one who despite it all,
is exactly who they were meant to be.

18ᵀᴴ MAY

'It's Alright'

When your heart is a little broken
despite time it never fully heals,
it's alright to shed some tears,
the loss you feel is real.

Life is a mixed bag of emotions
challenges, tests, and grief along the way,
it's alright to express your emotions,
tomorrow will be a brighter day.

19ᵀᴴ MAY

'Spirit'

Spirit: Meaning breath, it's our momentary living
it controls our mind and our body,
it's self-loving and self-giving.

It helps us to relax, to recover and to renew
focus on your breath,
it will re-balance you.

20TH MAY

'Collaborate'

Through collaboration
so much more can be achieved,
a collection of ideas,
that great minds have conceived.

Success can be shared
it's not meant for only one,
the sky would remain dark,
if only one star ever shone.

Reach out to others
connect and collaborate,
your goal is attainable,
go for it, don't hesitate.

21ST MAY

It takes being let down
to appreciate those who lift us up.

Be a lifter.

22ND MAY

'Trust'

Trust is a mutual bond
as we walk through life together,
if broken there will be a shadow,
which will remain forever.

Trust is a blessing
it needs to be cherished,
it's delicate, it requires respect,
to prevent it from being perished.

When you have trust in your life
there will always be someone there for you,
remember trust needs to be reciprocated,
gift it back, to those who gift it to you.

23ᴿᴰ MAY

Those warrior wings
that you carry so well,
they hold more weight
than you could ever tell.

Your strength inspires people
you have an ability to heal,
you are an energy being,
continue to empathetically feel.

24TH MAY

When negative self-talk creeps in and
you question your capability,
remember all you have endured,
has developed an abundance of ability.

25ᵀᴴ MAY

'Be'

Listen to the birds as they happily sing,
watch the branches and the leaves
as they gently swing.

Happiness can be found in the little things
we just need to awaken and to see,
take each moment a little easier,
allow more moments to 'be'.

26ᵀᴴ MAY

Sometimes progress can feel too slow
remember every success story
takes time to sustainably grow.

27ᵀᴴ MAY

'Positivity'

Positivity is seeing the good
even through a cloudy phase,
it's continuing to focus on the light,
just visible through the haze.

It's believing that good awaits
it's within arm's reach for us all,
it's overcoming every obstacle,
being proud and standing tall.

Positivity it keeps us focused
on what our goals are,
all we desire can be achieved,
the distance is never too far.

Hold onto positivity
let it be in every decision you make,
your positivity will be transparent,
in every step you take.

28TH MAY

'Remember the Time'

Remember the time, the friendship
the laughter and the fun,
remember the time, the beach,
the sand, the music, and the sun.

Remember the time as your lips curl
smiling with delight,
remembering the time, you light up,
your aura it glows bright.

Make time to remember the time
there is always much to appreciate,
with many more memory making days,
in the weeks ahead, you shall create.

29TH MAY

Through all that you continually do
don't forget to pause and make
a little time for you.

30TH MAY

'Words'

Our words they are powerful
they can generate both love and pain,
those feelings they can heal or scar,
the imprint can forever remain.

Words are a beautiful gift
allowing us to freely express,
a form of self-therapy,
which helps release our daily stress.

Words can have great impact
they can lift or rock your inner core,
aim to let only the positive in,
let negativity bounce off your armour.

Don't let the words of others deter you
remain strong in your own truth,
your grit and your persistence,
will always bear the sweetest fruit.

31ST MAY

If it was easy,
there would be no growth
in achieving it.

IST JUNE

A new month, new beginnings, a month of change
new opportunities, new relationships exchanged.

A new month which brings us to the half year
opening the gateway to more sunshine and cheer.

Just as it is with nature in June
in this new month you will inwardly bloom.

We welcome you June, we are blessed to see you
let your days feel lighter and filled with warmth too.

We are ready to receive all you will bring
as you gift us Summer and close the door on Spring.

2ND JUNE

'Keep Going'

Our journey requires resilience
ongoing determination to get us through,
keep going despite the challenges
know that you have the strength within you.

Keep going even when it feels
like the gradient is too steep,
take a break, pause a little
and then really breathe in deep.

When you are following your true passion
and reaching your goal feels close,
it's then that the momentum to keep going
really matters the most.

3RD JUNE

'Bluebells and Butterflies'

The lavender blue filled fields
sheer beauty, a collection of dreams,
butterflies perched peacefully on the bluebells tip,
delicately and angelically, they lovingly sit.

The relationship between them needs no words
they come from two inter-connecting worlds,
of nature, of earth, of growth and of living,
through their vibrancy, they keep on giving.

The bluebells and butterflies, they are Heaven sent
when you see them make wishes with intent,
those wishes will be heard loud and clear,
for it is angels that they both, represent.

4ᵀᴴ JUNE

'Celebrate'

Celebrate every win you achieve
no matter if the win is big or small,
every win is a success,
be proud of them all.

5TH JUNE

Life isn't about the wealth we build around us,
it's about the wealth we build within us.

6ᵀᴴ JUNE

No goal or vision is ever too big.
It's our own mindset which limits us.

Reset your mind, believe in yourself,
for your potential is limitless.

7ᵀᴴ JUNE

'Reflection'

Our reflection, the story of our life
every blemish, every facial line,
created through our life events,
representing the passage of time.

Take a moment to study your reflection
to recognise how magnificent you are,
your reflection carries a determination,
which has brought you safely, this far.

8ᵀᴴ JUNE

Love with all your soul.
Feel with all your heart.
Live gratefully through every breath.

9ᵀᴴ JUNE

'Steps'

Every step we take is
onward progression,
each one leads us towards
our own succession.

Take new steps mindfully
in the direction of your vision,
step onwards with confidence,
fulfil your purpose and your ambition.

10TH JUNE

'Values'

Your values are what makes you, 'you',
intrinsically linked to the career you pursue.

Those values, will guide you in all that you do
let that passion for your values, always shine through.

IITH JUNE

'Flowers'

Resemble the Summer flowers,
vibrantly standing tall and in full bloom,
showcase your authentic self,
as you brighten up every room.

12TH JUNE

Never let the challenges stall you
make you feel inferior or weak,
always use your voice for better
be the difference that you seek.

13TH JUNE

It's silent, then you hear a whisper
it shrouds you in warmth and love,
it's comforting and welcomed,
reassurance that you are guided from above.

Not every day is bright and breezy
some are cloudy, heavy, and hazy,
when that whisper comes your way,
know that tomorrow will be a brighter day.

14TH JUNE

Not everyone will be an advocate
that is perfectly fine,
the right people will enter your life,
at the divinely perfect time.

15TH JUNE

'Encouragement'

It feels good to encourage others
to support and to recognise,
we all need uplifting words,
to help us keep going and to rise.

Keep encouragement on your daily agenda
kind words can have a powerful impact,
when you encourage others,
that's what you will also attract.

16ᵀᴴ JUNE

'Soar'

As free as a bird in the open sky
spread out your wings and aim to fly high,
a fast rise doesn't give you time to explore,
go gently, enjoy the journey
and gracefully soar.

17ᵀᴴ JUNE

May you be blessed in many ways today
may any worries and doubts, drift away.

May you have a little time to show yourself some love
may you seek solace from nature and the skies above.

May the days ahead, in every way, be brighter
may you feel content and happy
and your mind much lighter.

18ᵀᴴ JUNE

'What matters the most'

What matters the most are our people
their love forever binds,
our family, our friends, those who care,
they are jewels of a very rare kind.

Give thanks for those special beings
who make every step we walk worthwhile,
whose presence uplifts in every way,
who help us to remember the warmth of a smile.

What matters the most are our people
earth angels, each and every one,
through the rain they bring us rainbows
and within us they unearth our sun.

19ᵀᴴ JUNE

'Sometimes'

Sometimes I wonder how I ended up here
I ponder and ask where have the years gone?
Time it seems to speed up with age,
the days and weeks they roll into one.

Sometimes I think of my mortality
of how fragile life can be,
then I reflect and give thanks,
for every day I get to see.

Sometimes the journey can get strange
we can get caught up in trivial things,
create space for a little relaxation,
feel the wellness benefits that it brings.

20TH JUNE

'Perhaps'

Perhaps the path is pre-ordained
perhaps it's our faith which needs maintained.

Perhaps we are blessed more than we even know
perhaps it's kindness we need to consistently show.

Perhaps our mission is to create a lasting peace
perhaps we can make inequality cease.

Perhaps we are the ones that our tomorrows need
perhaps now is the time to sow those seeds.

21ST JUNE

'Become'

The beauty of life is we can 'become'
anything which our soul desires,
with self-belief and determination,
the realisation of our goals can be acquired.

No matter where you are on your journey
your 'become' can be attained,
take the required action,
don't give up or refrain.

Our 'become' can change as life evolves
every chapter delivering something new,
whatever each chapter presents,
adapt and achieve the best 'become' for you.

22ND JUNE

'The Whispers'

Can you hear the whispers?
Vibrations that reach your very core,
they are softly spoken,
often easy to ignore.

Those whispers tell a story
offering advice to support your vision,
those whispers are subtle messages,
intuitively guiding your earthly mission.

Listen to those whispers
better advice is difficult to find,
all the answers you need are there,
in those whispers within your mind.

23RD JUNE

Dare to dream
like it's already here,
dare to pursue all that you wish for,
without any doubt or fear.

Dare to seize every opportunity
that will come your way,
dare to believe that something wonderful,
will appear in your life today.

24ᵀᴴ JUNE

Never allow anyone's behaviour
to shake your inner peace,
breathe, slow everything down,
feel the negative energy release.

Your wellbeing is too important
take the best possible care of you,
keep peace within every thought
and in everything that you do.

25ᵀᴴ JUNE

When the atmosphere is heavy
it's making way for the new,
keep your thoughts on your higher purpose
lighter days are ahead for you.

26TH JUNE

'Possible'

Possible, is everything that your mind can conceive
possible, is believing that your goal can be achieved.

Possible, is the equilibrium between faith and fear
possible is a vision that is vibrant and clear.

Possible, is knowing that 'impossible' isn't true
possible is understanding that the differential is 'you'.

27ᵀᴴ JUNE

Words can wound, words can heal,
take time to consider how your words
will make recipients feel.

28TH JUNE

Create time to spend on
what you love to do,
create room in your life
for something new.

Create energy that others
can feel and embrace,
create moments to enjoy
your own company and space.

Create time to listen
to become self-aware,
create time to take
the necessary self-care.

29TH JUNE

When at times it feels overwhelming
reflect on all you have already come through,
no matter what is ahead in the distance
the power to overcome is deep-set within you.

30ᵀᴴ JUNE

Don't aspire to be in someone else's league,
aspire to be in a league of your own.

1ST JULY

Hello July, the start of the
second half of the year,
may you bring us energy
that is positive and clear.

May you fill us with all
that our soul truly desires,
may you be uplifting and bright
and continuously inspire.

2ND JULY

'Self- Improvement'

You are your most important asset
continuous improvement is the key,
through knowledge, reading and listening,
your life purpose will be clearer to see.

Invest in all that you are
and all that you want to be,
self-improvement is a continuous journey,
enabling your ambitions to be set free.

3ᴿᴰ JULY

'Thrive'

You can't go back and change the past
now is all you have, aim to make the now last.

Be present and aware of who and where you are
reflect on all that you have accomplished thus far.

For now, in this moment, you are alive
it's time to release any inhibitions
and to gloriously thrive.

4TH JULY

'New Ideas'

Be aware of the new ideas
as they pop into your mind,
think about them all,
for creativity you might find.

Those ideas they have been sent to you
they could open a brand-new door,
don't instantly discount them,
research them and fully explore.

Embrace all those new ideas
review each one,
through acting on ideas,
a new begin can be won.

5TH JULY

Where there is love
there is always hope.

6ᵀᴴ JULY

'Where you are…'

Where you are should be harmonious
the people, the place, the vibe,
surrounded by those who encourage you,
who are always there by your side.

Where you are matters
it's where you invest your days,
the energy needs to raise you up,
to inspire you in a variety of ways.

7TH JULY

Become your own best friend
then watch as life shifts in your favour.

8ᵀᴴ JULY

'The Best Things in Life are Free'

The best things in life are free
the coffee roasting, the cup of tea,
with people, in whose company you love to be.

The fresh crisp air, the country walk
the scenery admired, while you talk.

The reminiscing of years gone by
the stories they all make you smile,

The best things in life are free
spend time with loved ones and be inspired to be.

9TH JULY

'Wonder'

Wonder are the tingles you get
as you envisage your goal becoming real,
when it becomes within arm's reach,
self-admiration is what you feel.

The wonder as your grit and dedication
makes your dreams come true,
your passion for all that you are
and all that you love to do.

Never lose that sense of wonder
it is how dreams are made,
may that wonder remain alive
and despite challenges, never fade.

10ᵀᴴ JULY

'Rest'

It's good to rest
to lift your feet off the ground,
to be still and tune in,
to every earthly sound.

Rest gives your whole self
time to rejuvenate,
put your wellbeing first,
everything else for now, can wait.

IITH JULY

Never underestimate the
healing power of a hug.

12ᵀᴴ JULY

'Shine'

Shine with all your
internal vibrance,
life is fragile,
freely dance.

Allow your talents to shine
let them naturally unfold,
your unique story,
through living is told.

Keep shining
know that you naturally glow,
enable your inner confidence,
to continually grow.

13ᵀᴴ JULY

Smile, there is so much to be thankful for
smile, focus on your blessings and not the chores.

Smile, every day brings in fresh new air
smile, it shows others that you care.

Smile, for positive energy surrounds you
smile, your persistence will deliver your break-through.

14ᵀᴴ JULY

When the energy feels heavy and strained
It's normal to feel a little weary and drained.

Quieten your mind, your body, and your spirit
stay in the now, engaged in this minute.

Always be aware of how you are feeling
talk to someone you trust and gain healing.

15ᵀᴴ JULY

'Morning feelings…'

Acknowledge how you feel
each morning as you rise,
take a few minutes, centre yourself,
breathe in the morning sky.

Be aware of your feelings
to the messages therein,
self-awareness is important,
to enable the new day to begin.

16ᵀᴴ JULY

'You Are Always More Than Enough'

You are here for a pre-ordained
amount of time,
it is an unknown period,
which no-one can define.

Step back and view your present
where you are today,
it's taken resilience and courage,
to make it all this way!

Next time you feel unworthy
or when life it seems too tough,
pause and take a step back,
for you are always more than enough.

17ᵀᴴ JULY

When you leave the door open for only
the good, the kind and the true,
you will no longer allow anyone to enter,
whose energy is unhealthy for you.

18ᵀᴴ JULY

Do the right thing in every situation
do the right thing, avoid unnecessary ramifications.

Do the right thing, it's always the best choice
do the right thing, use your words and your voice.

19ᵀᴴ JULY

One of our most impactful vulnerabilities
can be the intimidation of our own capabilities.

20TH JULY

'Obstacles'

Along this twisty road
many obstacles you will meet,
you can either navigate around them,
or stop and admit defeat.

Strength isn't gained
if we let the obstacles win,
every obstacle carries a message,
only learnt by not giving in!

No matter the amount of obstacles
that you encounter along the way,
you can overcome every one of them,
ahead of obstacles are calmer days.

21ˢᵀ JULY

'Maybe…'

Maybe all that you desire
is around the next bend,
maybe your expectations will be exceeded,
by what the Universe sends.

Maybe when we ask for something good
something great is what we get,
maybe we are never in control,
and it's wise never to fret.

Maybe we are already richer
than we can fully contemplate,
maybe all we need is to trust,
for our divine timing, is never late.

22ND JULY

'My Wish'

My wish is that you get
to fully enjoy every day,
my wish is that many blessings,
continue to come your way.

My wish is that your worries
are released into the air,
my wish is that faith gives you strength,
through any unforeseen despair.

My wish is as you look at your reflection
you see you are a beautiful gift,
my wish is that as we rise,
we give others a supportive lift.

23RD JULY

'Through the Eyes of a Child'

Through the eyes of a child
is an inclusive land,
through the eyes of a child,
we all walk hand in hand.

Through the eyes of a child
there are twinkling eyes and smiles,
through the eyes of a child,
there are blue skies for miles.

Through the eyes of a child
is pure love and peace,
through the eyes of a child,
is where we need to retreat.

24ᵀᴴ JULY

'Be Gentle'

Be gentle with yourself and
with those around you,
let love and compassion be shown,
through all you say and do.

Everything happens for a reason
allow yourself to gradually progress,
be extra gentle with yourself,
unleash all the unwelcomed stress.

Be gentle and let empathy
lead the way,
we all need a little tenderness,
to get us through the day.

25TH JULY

Even through challenge
so much can be achieved
keep going, have faith
and forever self-believe.

26TH JULY

Life is short
even if the road feels long
through every stumble,
you remain strong,
despite the hurdles,
you know you are where you belong.

27ᵀᴴ JULY

Behind every smile
is a story.

28TH JULY

If you could fully see
the magnificence of the light within,
you would never question
yourself again.

29TH JULY

When you realise how much time you spent worrying
about what might come your way,
you will have a refreshed perspective on time,
no longer allowing mind-based worries,
to take over the goodness of the day.

30ᵀᴴ JULY

'International Friendship Day'

Friends are like family
they brighten up our days,
they support us and cheer us on,
in a multitude of ways.

Friendship is a gift
precious and to be treasured,
give thanks for every friendship,
a blessing which cannot be measured.

31ST JULY

Let your body rest and totally be
let your mind empty and feel free,
let your breath be the only sound,
let self-love be refound.

1ST AUGUST

Welcome August
meaning; distinguished and illustrious,
may you gift opportunities,
so we can be industrious.

As you arrive, we ask
that you are extra kind,
helping us to replenish,
our peace of mind.

2ND AUGUST

'Reach Out'

Reach out to someone close to you today
a check-in to ensure that they are okay.

Talking and listening is a comfort for us all
reach out, send a message, make that call.

3ᴿᴰ AUGUST

Whilst the ego loves busy
the soul loves peace,
never get so busy doing,
that you forget to be.

4TH AUGUST

You are precious
you are gifted
you are strong
you are loved
you bring light
you belong.

5ᵀᴴ AUGUST

If you push too hard, exhaustion will call
if it does, take a break, it's okay to stall.

Our whole self needs lots of tender loving care
step outside, fill up your lungs with fresh, clean air.

Exhaustion can fatigue the mind
take it easy and to your body, be kind.

6ᵀᴴ AUGUST

When a decision, excites you
and simultaneously scares you,
close your eyes and let your intuition
guide you as to what you should do.

7ᵀᴴ AUGUST

With every onward step you take
a more peaceful life you will create.

8ᵀᴴ AUGUST

'Stuff'

Through life we accumulate
so much stuff,
its only when you sift through it,
you realise you have so much.

Stuff, is made up of
material things,
it's not the stuff
which gives our soul wings.

Stuff is replaceable,
people and memories are not,
it's joy and love which are important,
not how much stuff we've got.

9ᵀᴴ AUGUST

Silence the self-critic,
give a voice to self-praise.

10ᵀᴴ AUGUST

Write down every ambition
that your mind conceives,
write down the ideal outcome,
that you want to achieve.

Write down the path
you really want to take,
write down all the choices,
that only you can make.

11TH AUGUST

You decide the life
you wish to lead,
you determine the
direction and the speed.

12ᵀᴴ AUGUST

Never be afraid to be authentic
and to do your thing,
for your heart was always meant to dance
and your soul was born to sing.

13TH AUGUST

This day is momentous
never again to be repeated
remember every day you survived,
when you thought you'd been defeated.

Today can be everything
you would love it to be,
be grateful for every day
that you are destined to see.

14ᵀᴴ AUGUST

Remember, no-one is you,
let that fact guide you in all that you do.

15ᵀᴴ AUGUST

'Change'

Change, it surrounds us
all change moves us swiftly along,
some changes they light us up,
for others we need to be strong.

Every change happens for a reason
aligned to where we are needed to go,
know that changes enter,
to allow your purpose to more freely flow.

Change opens new doors
assertively walk through,
for on the other side of change,
great things shall be waiting for you.

16ᵀᴴ AUGUST

Always keep your precious people near
for so much can change in a day,
a week, a month, and a year.

17ᵀᴴ AUGUST

'I Did It All My Way'

None of us know the moment
none of us know the day,
so, rejoice in the beauty,
of this earth in which we stay.

Surround yourself with happiness
people, places, and things,
spend your time with only those,
who truly give you wings.

For when the bright light calls you
you can honestly say,
'I lived a life filled with joy,
I did it all my way'.

18ᵀᴴ AUGUST

Always follow your heart
it's okay to pursue something new,
take a leap of faith,
it will revitalise you.

19TH AUGUST

Our wellbeing is achieved
from the inside out,
it begins in the mind,
with what we think about.

You are in control of your
thoughts and journey,
you hold the pen,
write a memorable story.

20ᵀᴴ AUGUST

We all light up when we talk
about something that we love to do,
whatever that is do more of it!

21ST AUGUST

When you focus
on your wellbeing,
you are taking action
towards being well.

22ND AUGUST

We are never alone as we walk through life
we meet fellow warriors through our strife,
always believe that brighter pastures await
have courage, be brave and, above all, have faith.

23RD AUGUST

Emotions are a sign of passion, love, and strength.
They are not a sign of weakness.

24ᵀᴴ AUGUST

It takes an abundance of rainwater
for the most beautiful flowers to grow,
so don't get disheartened,
when growth is a little slow.

The sturdiest of foliage
took its time to bloom,
the pace of growth varies,
dependent upon the envisioned room.

Grow at your own individual speed
perfection it takes time,
trust that you are growing at the correct rate
and that success will be thine!

25ᵀᴴ AUGUST

Even when life gets uncertain
we can still enjoy the view,
keep living and loving the present,
don't let uncertainty inhibit you.

26ᵀᴴ AUGUST

'An Angel Whispered in My Ear'

An angel whispered in my ear
'come sit a while with me,
I know it's been a turbulent time
and the path it is difficult to see.

Rest dear one and clear your mind
it will all become quite clear,
I am here always by your side,
remember there's nothing to fear.

You are unique a blessed gift
no-one is like you,
your heart it is wide open,
you're authentic, kind, and true.

I ask that you remember
how special you really are,
you can overcome the onward journey,
given what you have endured thus far.'

An angel whispered in my ear
I feel their presence still,
I've gained strength to face what lies ahead,
for I know it's all God's will.

27ᵀᴴ AUGUST

Don't block or fear success
you've worked hard,
you deserve only the best.

28ᵀᴴ AUGUST

Carry hope in your heart
and love and laughter in your soul,
sprinkle your inspiration,
everywhere you go.

29ᵀᴴ AUGUST

Sometimes we need to say sorry
to ourselves,
for putting up with situations,
that we never deserved.

30ᵀᴴ AUGUST

Turn frustration into motivation
take a chance and make a change.
When you wholeheartedly believe,
it's amazing what you can achieve.

31ST AUGUST

Month endings
create new beginnings,
new opportunities,
new ways of being.

Just like the seasons
we continually change,
we evolve, we develop,
we turn a new page.

Autumn is coming
release the old,
your best days,
are yet to unfold.

1ST SEPTEMBER

This new month
step over the fear
and into courage.

Move fearlessly forwards.

2ᴺᴰ SEPTEMBER

We will experience moments
which will raise us to new heights,
we will experience moments,
filled with love and light.

We will experience moments
which will test us to our core,
we will experience moments,
questioning what this is all for.

We will experience moments
sparking an array of feelings,
all those moments,
gives our life its meaning.

3RD SEPTEMBER

Remember, rainbows usually appear after a storm.
Hold on, your rainbow is coming.

4ᵀᴴ SEPTEMBER

'Take it Slow'

Throughout the day
it can be difficult to take it slow,
yet we can't sustain days of all
go, go, go.

Pause, even if only for a minute
to really feel your breath,
reconnect to yourself,
there is no need to fret.

Along this journey self-love is needed
to help us safely along the road,
take it slow, rest for a while,
create opportunities to lighten your load.

5TH SEPTEMBER

May each of us remember to say,
'life is lived moment to moment
and day by day'.

6TH SEPTEMBER

Every second is a blessing
cherish each one,
today's to-do list,
it will eventually get done!

7TH SEPTEMBER

'You are Amazing'

When our hearts are heavy
we question all that we are,
we can be our own worst critic,
reopening every internal scar.

Life is filled with tests
which takes resilience to overcome,
those tests are lessons
and you've learned from every-one.

It's time to silence the critic
be proud of your journey so far,
heal those scars, give yourself praise,
you are amazing, just as you are.

8ᵀᴴ SEPTEMBER

'The Future is Bright'

It's been like a rollercoaster
you often wonder why,
yet every bird has practice runs,
before they eventually fly!

Every stumble has made you stronger
you are now ready to take flight,
trust in the power of your own wings,
the path is clear, and the future is bright.

9TH SEPTEMBER

When you radiate your positive energy
through everything you do,
you'll be surprised at who is out there,
needing someone just like you.

10TH SEPTEMBER

Out of the darkness, appears the light
after the day, follows the night,
with a fighting spirit, life truly glows,
with prayer and faith, positivity flows.

We are all on this journey of bumps and bends
none of us knowing when the journey will end,
be sure to make your dreams come true,
one life, once chance, it's all up to you.

11TH SEPTEMBER

Your mind is your powerhouse
reset it as often as you need,
aim to be mind-conscious,
momentarily stop and really breathe.

12TH SEPTEMBER

'Inner Peace'

Allow tranquillity and peace
to slowly flow through you,
as you recentre and settle,
you will know what you need to do.

Replenishing that inner peace
on any given day,
will more ably assist you,
to navigate your way.

13TH SEPTEMBER

'Have Faith'

I've known sadness, I've known pain
maintaining faith, I've risen again.

Life is filled with twists, turns, and bends
we wade through with the help,
of our family and friends.

Never let life's journey dimmish your light
hold on, have faith, it will be alright.

Around the next corner is something new
welcome it and absorb the incredible view.

Beauty surrounds us, everywhere we go
that beauty is within, have faith to let it show.

14TH SEPTEMBER

'Wishes'

Wishing is a magical feeling
it puts a smile upon your face,
when your thoughts drift to a wish,
it elevates you to a wonderful place.

Keep on wishing
for wishes do come true,
the next wish to be granted,
could be especially for you.

15ᵀᴴ SEPTEMBER

'Blessings'

As we acknowledge our blessings
a gateway opens to attract more,
our higher vibrational being,
creates an unlimited forest to explore.

Our blessings they begin
the second we open our eyes,
we are blessed each morning,
when we get to see the sun rise.

Really count your blessings
be aware and clearly see,
the more you count your blessings,
the more abundant you will be.

16ᵀᴴ SEPTEMBER

'Thank You'

Thank you for the love around me
and the love deep in my heart,
thank you for the blustery storms,
which have helped to clear my path.

Thank you for all the gifts
that have been bestowed upon me,
thank you for my hopes and dreams,
and for giving me clarity.

Thank you for the experiences
even the days that made me sore,
they shaped me into a better person,
I now know what my purpose is for.

As I walk onwards
I know you hold my hand,
I am awake to your guidance
and I trust in your divine plan.

17ᵀᴴ SEPTEMBER

'Patience'

The best things in life take time
patience is the key,
all that is meant to arrive,
you will eventually see.

Keep focused on your desired outcome
feel it, like it's already here,
keep going and keep growing,
pursue and persevere.

Patience is a daily ritual
life is not meant to be fast paced,
all that you are working towards,
will be worth every hurdle, you have faced!

18TH SEPTEMBER

'Make a Promise'

Make a promise to recognise
the person you have become,
make a promise to enjoy life,
to laugh and have some fun.

Make a promise to remove
anything which is unhealthy for you,
make a promise to love yourself
and all that you choose to do.

Make a promise to notice the good
even when the darkness appears,
make a promise to be thankful,
for every day you get to spend here.

19TH SEPTEMBER

'Take a Seat'

Take a seat
a little time to be still,
it can often feel,
like a very steep hill.

Take a seat
raise your feet off the ground,
tap into the faith,
which you have found.

Take a seat
it will be okay,
if in doubt,
close your eyes and pray.

Take a seat
the path is clear,
those times you long for,
are almost here.

20ᵀᴴ SEPTEMBER

'Clouds'

Behind the clouds, the sun rests
its shadows around us fall
with the clouds continuous movement,
eventually the sun will shine on us all.

Clouds resemble our journey
like the sun we too need rest
when we slowly reappear,
we will be feeling our very best.

If it feels a little cloudy
know that your sun is on the way
tomorrow brings a new dawn,
a new sunrise, a new day.

21ST SEPTEMBER

'Please Remember'

Please remember there is a light around you
it's as bright as it can be,
know that it is there,
even though it's not visible to see.

Please remember that you are cared for
maybe more than you currently know,
please remember it takes courage,
to let raw emotions, show.

Please remember, down days don't last
it's okay not to feel okay,
please remember that much better days,
are always on their way.

22ND SEPTEMBER

Your spirit wants you
to feel happy and free,
self-connect, daydream,
take time to be.

We are here for a reason
we are part of a Universal plan,
even when you feel like you can't,
know that you can.

Allow your spirit to gain freedom
don't be bashful and shy,
you are here to really flourish,
allow your spirit to fly high.

23RD SEPTEMBER

'Attract'

Attract all that you truly want
keep all thoughts positive and bright,
wrap yourself up,
in only love and light.

Focus on all that you have
with a grateful heart,
remember gratitude is how,
attraction really starts.

24TH SEPTEMBER

Your life resembles a masterpiece
you are holding the pencil,
keep creating, keep designing,
for you are the stencil.

25TH SEPTEMBER

Add a little rejuvenation time
silence the overthinking,
time which transports you,
becoming unaware that you are blinking.

Schedule daily time in the diary
to enter that rejuvenation space,
it's always time well spent,
to go to that meditative place.

26ᵀᴴ SEPTEMBER

'Nature'

Nature has a way of grounding us
when we inhale all its glory,
its changing beauty continues,
to tell its own story.

Nature never seems hindered
by the environment it is in,
it releases, adapts and relentlessly,
recreates itself again.

We can learn so much from nature
of how powerful and agile it can be,
we are so much like nature,
may we feel empowered to always see.

27TH SEPTEMBER

'Good Thoughts'

Try to notice the good thoughts
that enter your mind,
those which are uplifting,
self-worthy and kind.

Protect your precious energy
from self-doubts and fear,
good thoughts fuel positive energy,
keeping the mind focused and clear.

Become conscious of your thoughts
silence those that drain you,
you deserve to feel happy,
allow only good thoughts through.

28TH SEPTEMBER

'Let's Talk'

Let's talk about how we feel
talking really helps us to heal.

Let's talk about all that's going on
let's support each other to remain strong.

Let's break the stigma, talking is freeing
and it is an essential element of our wellbeing.

29ᵀᴴ SEPTEMBER

'Feelings'

Honour your feelings, every single one
understand the trigger they've been derived from.

Your feelings are important, acknowledge them all
none of them are irrelevant, petty, or small.

Your feelings matter, they are a part of you
be kind to yourself, it's important that you do.

30TH SEPTEMBER

With yourself, don't be so tough,
your best is always good enough.

IST OCTOBER

A new month
new possibilities
new connections
new experiences
new memories
a new mindset.

2ND OCTOBER

'A Little Time'

A little time to relax, to simply be
a little time, a coffee, a cup of tea.

A little time, a magazine, a book
a little time, a boxset that will get you hooked!

A little time, lounging in your snuggly seat
a little time listening to your favourite beat.

A little time, a little self-care just for you
a little time to unwind, to be and not do!

3RD OCTOBER

'What If'

What if all that you wish for,
is on the other side of fear,
what if the doors you seek to open
are already very near?

What if people are praising you,
you simply cannot hear,
what if there are no barriers
and the future path is clear?

4TH OCTOBER

When you are open to receiving all that is good,
don't be surprised if what you get is great!

5TH OCTOBER

'World Teachers Day'

Today we celebrate all teachers
a special group of people they all are,
the knowledge they consistently instil,
enables us to go far.

Through their hands greatness is created
they inspire everyone in the room,
teachers, thank you for helping us to learn,
to self-believe and to fully bloom.

6TH OCTOBER

'Have you ever…?'

Have you ever taken the time
to really self-praise?
Have you ever looked at yourself
and adoringly gaze?

Have you ever viewed your body
as a vessel filled with capability?
Have you ever understood
your own vulnerability?

Have you ever stopped to acknowledge
everything that you are?
It's time to fully love yourself,
for you are a magnificent star.

7ᵀᴴ OCTOBER

Multi-tasking is overrated,
take it one task at a time.

8ᵀᴴ OCTOBER

The more you try,
the more you learn.

The more you learn,
the more you grow.

The more you grow,
the brighter you glow.

9TH OCTOBER

It's okay to press pause,
to put your feet up and to rest.

10TH OCTOBER

'World Mental Health Day'

If you are struggling
and finding it difficult to cope,
reach out for support,
for there is always hope.

IITH OCTOBER

'Footprints'

Every footprint that you choose to take
leads you closer to the life
that you wish to make.

Your footprints are distinctive to you
each one directs you towards
all you endeavour to do.

Make each footprint with determination
you will eventually arrive
at your desired destination.

12TH OCTOBER

'Day by Day'

Little by little, day by day
What's meant to be, will find its way.

Don't overthink, don't over plan
simply do, all that you can.

Little by little, day by day
it will all work out, it will be okay.

13TH OCTOBER

Inner strength doesn't come from
navigating along straight roads,
it comes from every unforeseen
roadblock that was successfully overcome.

14TH OCTOBER

We never know how or when
our journey ceases here,
make every earthly moment count
and keep your loved ones near.

15TH OCTOBER

No amount of money can buy a minute of time.
Time is our most valuable commodity.
Spend your time wisely.

16ᵀᴴ OCTOBER

Never underestimate the power of positivity.

Positive thoughts,
positive words,
and positive actions,
create a more positive life.

17TH OCTOBER

Through your life
through your career,
in everything you do,
spend your time with only those,
who truly value you.

18ᵀᴴ OCTOBER

It's not how gracefully we fall,
it's how gracefully we rise.

19TH OCTOBER

Failure often leads us to greater success
we gain wisdom to help us achieve our best,
stand tall and be proud of all that you are
despite challenges, you have made it this far.

20ᵀᴴ OCTOBER

'Around the Next Bend'

Around the next bend there is so much to see
rolling hills, green fields, amazing scenery.

Around the next bend, the sky is blue and clear
the clouds have dispersed the sun reappears.

May hope be with you, may your faith never end
soon you will be, around the next bend.

21ST OCTOBER

'As I Rise'

As I rise, I sit on the side of the bed
I become aware of all the thoughts inside my head.

I close my eyes for a minute or two
I ask myself 'what thoughts are the ones that
will see me through?'

I climb into my mind, and I flip the script
I visualise images which give me a lift.

I am in control of all that I think, feel, and do
today, whatever you have in store,
I am now ready for you!

22ND OCTOBER

When you pause you realise
materially you need very little,
all you need is love, support and peace.

23ᴿᴰ OCTOBER

Restore that sense of calm
from the inside out,
reflect on what this life,
is all about.

We all have a purpose
each and every one,
at times we can forget,
busy getting things done.

Reconnect with all
that is important to you,
let calmness re-enter,
recharge and renew.

24TH OCTOBER

Remind yourself of how great you are
you have all you need to get you through,
remind yourself that everything is temporary
and better times are ahead of you.

25TH OCTOBER

Inner resilience comes from many places
but usually, it comes from events
we were never prepared for.

26ᵀᴴ OCTOBER

A new dawn
a new day,
may the light shine,
to guide the way.

27TH OCTOBER

Sometimes bravery is digging deeper
than you ever imagined
in pursuit of your dreams.

28TH OCTOBER

'The Climb'

Some days the climb it can get tough
you ask yourself if you are good enough.

Some days the climb will test your patience
this is when you utilise your well of resilience.

The climb can be achieved as you see fit
step by step, you can conquer it.

Don't force it or rush it, you know your limit
when it comes to the climb, don't ever quit!

29ᵀᴴ OCTOBER

It's not about what is happening to you
it's how you cope with what's
happening to you
that really matters.

30ᵀᴴ OCTOBER

We can't predict the future
we can't go back to the past,
all we have is now,
aim to make the now last.

31ST OCTOBER

The calmer you are,
the calmer your life becomes.

1ST NOVEMBER

Hello November
the 11th month begins,
you can bring rain and
occasionally high winds.

Some days your sun beams
providing much needed light,
your autumnal colours are so
vibrant and bright.

November, no matter how
turbulent it gets outside,
let the warmth in our hearts,
continue to be our guide.

2ND NOVEMBER

'Let All Worry Go'

Close your eyes slow everything down
let all worry go,
there's no need to dwell on the past,
try to let today, naturally flow.

Don't question the how
take gentle steps, today and every day,
what's meant to arrive in your life,
is already on its way.

Make a commitment to yourself
to let all worry go,
replace it with confidence in who you are,
for you are more gifted than perhaps you know.

3RD NOVEMBER

'Health'

Today do a self-check
revise your wellbeing and your health,
your ongoing wellness,
is your greatest source of wealth.

Your nutrition, your exercise
your overall health regime,
can only be found in
your daily routine.

Evaluate your health
you need to be at your best,
remember it's also important
to sleep well and to rest.

4ᵀᴴ NOVEMBER

The greatest work
that you can ever do,
is aligning the passion,
purpose and peace within you.

5ᵀᴴ NOVEMBER

Take time to
acknowledge your own greatness,
recognise the difference that you make
to your family, friends, colleagues, clients,
community and to the world.

You are the difference.

6TH NOVEMBER

'Be Open'

Be open to every opportunity
that is presented to you,
walk through the doors
that lead to the new.

Be open to the support
which will be offered when you ask,
be open to succeeding
with any given task.

Be open to the new connections
you will make through time,
be open to believing
that this is your time to shine.

7ᵀᴴ NOVEMBER

'No Limits'

If you had no perceived limits
what would you do?
The calling of your heart,
that speaks to you.

Envisage no limits
to realising your dreams,
allow your wisdom to flow,
like a clear water stream.

Live like there are no limits
what you seek you will find,
for those limits only exist,
deep inside your mind.

8ᵀᴴ NOVEMBER

'The Dawn'

As the dawn awakes us, a fresh day arrives
a date never to be repeated, again in our lives.

A new chance to create, to do our best
seize the day, release yesterday's stress.

The dawn always rises, proudly in the sky
let every dawn remind us, to aim high.

9ᵀᴴ NOVEMBER

'You Can'

You can get over every bump in the road
you can lean on others when you need to offload.

You can succeed, with effort and commitment
you can allow yourself, to feel excitement.

You can do everything that makes your life fulfilling
you can, for you are an incredible, human being.

10ᵀᴴ NOVEMBER

Recalling happy memories
can put a smile on your face,
they can instantly take you,
to a magical place.

Reminisce about those memories
reconnect with that joy once more,
the wonderful thing about memories,
is that there are always new ones to explore!

11ᵀᴴ NOVEMBER

'Time to 'Talk'

Make time to talk
to family, a colleague, or a friend,
let them know that in tough times,
upon you, they can depend.

Talking is sharing
it helps to calm the mind,
a listening ear is so important,
to someone you trust and who is kind.

Make time to talk today
let the conversation flow,
the words that you will speak and hear,
will gently soothe your soul.

12ᵀᴴ NOVEMBER

Stay centred and remain authentic and true
let all unnecessary stress
be washed away from you.

13ᵀᴴ NOVEMBER

'World Kindness Day'

Kindness is our gift to give
it's shown through the life we live.
A smile, a wave, the simple things,
to others, great joy they can bring.

Let's spread kindness among us all
let's help one another if we fall.
Wear kindness like a coat, for all to see
the best thing about kindness, is it's free.

14ᵀᴴ NOVEMBER

'Waves'

Life can resemble waves,
some days are calm and still,
others, they are more powerful
it feels like you're sprinting uphill.

But all days, like waves, are temporary,
resilience is built throughout them all,
tap into that lake of bravery,
you may stumble, but you will not fall.

15ᵀᴴ NOVEMBER

'You are a Warrior'

You have already experienced so much.

Hurt, loss, sadness, pain.

Emotions can hit you without warning and that's okay.

The heaviness will pass.

You are equipped for all the days that
you will be granted.

You are a survivor.

You are a torchbearer.

You are a warrior.

16ᵀᴴ NOVEMBER

Aim to live, with the ability to understand
it may not always be how you imagined,
but know that it's all part of your earthly plan.

Learn every day, soak life in
every day is a new chance,
a new opportunity to start again.

17ᵀᴴ NOVEMBER

'Empathy'

Everyone's journey varies
we can only walk in our own shoes,
empathy is important,
to respect each other's views.

Be grateful if your journey is easier
than those you walk alongside,
understand that for so many,
it can be a turbulent ride.

A more empathetic world
together we can make,
through empathy, care, and compassion,
a nicer land we will create.

18ᵀᴴ NOVEMBER

As you awaken to this new day
let all that built up stress go,
new horizons are in sight,
you are braver than you know.

It's not about the speed
it requires your patience,
being extra loving with yourself,
will build future resilience.

You are your own master
take each stride carefully,
you don't need to move faster,
you need to progress mindfully.

Through time you will reflect
and be proud of all that you are,
pause and really catch a breath,
you are destined to go far.

19ᵀᴴ NOVEMBER

Life is a series of highs and lows.

During the high times, remain humble,
during the low times, remain hopeful.

20ᵀᴴ NOVEMBER

It's okay to put your emotions out there
tears are therapy, it shows that you care.

You give so much of yourself in all that you do
it's time to put yourself first and to take care of you.

21ST NOVEMBER

When you forget how amazing you are
I hope you have a wonderful circle of people,
who lovingly remind you.

22ND NOVEMBER

When you feel tired
go gently, do only what you need to do,
it's self-kindness and self-love
that will help to get you through.

23RD NOVEMBER

'Never Give Up'

Every best outcome develops
from the most arduous of times,
we gain a drive to keep going,
believing all will eventually realign.

Never give up on something
that you truly desire,
the story of how you made it happen,
will indefinitely inspire.

24ᵀᴴ NOVEMBER

May the love in your heart
always light up your face,
may you approach each day
with positivity and grace.

25ᵀᴴ NOVEMBER

Perhaps it's not simply the fear of failure
but also, the fear of success,
which act as a foundation
for self-doubt.

26TH NOVEMBER

If you wait for the perfect time
you shall eternally wait,
now is the only time that's guaranteed
take action, don't hesitate.

27TH NOVEMBER

Life is so short
rise up to every gifted day,
release old hurts
let optimism pave the way.

28TH NOVEMBER

It takes courage to look inside ourselves
to understand the workings of the mind,
through that self-investment
so many answers you will find.

29ᵀᴴ NOVEMBER

When things don't happen
as you thought they would or should,
it's because something much better
and more joyous, is on the way.

30ᵀᴴ NOVEMBER

Immerse yourself in becoming
all that you want to be,
commit, be all in,
positive self-impact you will soon see.

IST DECEMBER

'Hello December'

Hello December, the pathway to Christmas
taking us to the end of the year,
December we are glad to see you
a new beginning is once again near.

Hello December, sprinkle your magic
into everyone's home,
let that Christmas magic follow us
everywhere we roam.

Hello December, we truly believe
joyous news you will bring,
like the festive carol singers
may we all harmoniously sing.

2ND DECEMBER

It's not about how much money is in the home,
it's about how much love is in the home.

3RD DECEMBER

Breathe in self-acceptance,
breathe out self-doubt.

4ᵀᴴ DECEMBER

Rest, replenish and renew,
as often as you need to.

5TH DECEMBER

You are in full control of your destiny,
never give anyone else that power.

6TH DECEMBER

No matter what comes your way
never give up or give in,
every dawn and every day
is a chance to start again.

7TH DECEMBER

'Capabilities'

Always believe in your
abundance of capabilities,
the talents that you naturally possess,
contain unlimited possibilities.

Move forwards with faith
in all that you are,
you are capable and gifted,
you are a uniquely beautiful star.

8TH DECEMBER

Tune in and listen to your inner instinct,
it will always speak honestly to you.

9ᵀᴴ DECEMBER

Trust that all is good
continue working towards your vision,
inspire all those that you engage with
for that's an important part of your mission.

10ᵀᴴ DECEMBER

When you question how far you can go
to make your dreams come true,
reflect on how far you've come
every mile has been travelled by you.

11ᵀᴴ DECEMBER

Christmas is a magical season
the goodwill is wonderful to see,
at this time of year
we all deserve to feel happy and free.

12TH DECEMBER

Today may your smile shine brightly
may your face warmly glow,
pass on that smile to all you meet
never be afraid to let your joyfulness show.

13TH DECEMBER

May love and joy light you up
may all stressors fall behind,
may every footprint you make be gentle
may every experience you have be kind.

14TH DECEMBER

It is the season that is usually filled
with lots of laughter and cheer,
but it can also be the time
when we miss those no longer here.

Be kind to yourself
it has been a very busy year,
spend time with those who lift your spirits
let the festive magic reappear.

15ᵀᴴ DECEMBER

Even through dark days
there is always light,
the heaviness will gradually pass
know that it will be alright.

16ᵀᴴ DECEMBER

With patience, hope and perseverance
all storms will eventually move on.

17ᵀᴴ DECEMBER

Let your love and light flow,
let all distress go.

18TH DECEMBER

A little time to power down
with those we hold dear,
is all that's really needed to enjoy
this magical time of year.

19ᵀᴴ DECEMBER

Have no regrets
be brave and see every new experience,
as an opportunity for self-improvement
and self-empowerment.

20ᵀᴴ DECEMBER

Sometimes the turbulence
helps to awaken you
to what is important.

Life is a blessing,
make a continual commitment to
appreciate every minute of it.

21ST DECEMBER

In life we can't help everyone
but we can always help someone.

Through giving
is how we truly receive.

22ND DECEMBER

'Burnout'

That exhausted feeling
your enthusiasm is strained,
it's the burnout calling
you're depleted and a little drained.

Never ignore those signs,
you need to feel healthy and well,
listen to your body
never ignore the burnout alarm bell.

23RD DECEMBER

It's only when you walk through
times of darkness,
that you appreciate and
value the light.

24ᵀᴴ DECEMBER

Let the magic be felt in the air
on this Christmas Eve,
look up to the sky, make a wish
and with all your heart, believe.

25TH DECEMBER

It's who is around the Christmas tree
that matters today,
may love and blessings
surround you in every way.

26TH DECEMBER

'A Little White Feather'

A little white feather appeared to me today
a reminder that those in Heaven are never far away.

It was as white as pure crisp snow
to all who have departed, our love continues to grow.

This little white feather I felt grateful to see
thank you dear loved one, for sending it to me.

27TH DECEMBER

Never get consumed with searching
for the extraordinary,
that you miss out on the pleasure found
in the ordinary.

28TH DECEMBER

As a new year approaches
carry love and light in your soul,
our world needs your presence
spread your positivity everywhere you go.

29ᵀᴴ DECEMBER

It's okay to speak your truth
it's okay to protect your energy,
It's okay to let go,
It's okay to change direction,
It's okay to follow your dreams.

30TH DECEMBER

Your future is what you dare
to believe it to be.

31ST DECEMBER

May your blessings be plenty
and your worries be few,
say goodbye to the old
prepare to receive the new.